HAL LEONARD *MORE* EASY POP RHYTHMS

GUITAR METHOD

Supplement to Any Guitar Method

T0058893

INTRODUCTION

Welcome to *Easy Pop Rhythms*, a collection of 20 pop and rock favorites arranged for easy guitar chord strumming. If you're a beginning guitarist, you've come to the right place. With the songs in this book, you can practice basic chords and strumming patterns—plus learn how to play 20 great tunes!

This book can be used on its own or as a supplement to any guitar method. If you're using it with the *Hal Leonard Guitar Method*, it coordinates with the chords and skills introduced in Book 2. Use the table of contents on page 3 to see what chords each song contains and to determine when you're ready to play a song.

ISBN 978-0-634-04157-0

7777 W. BLUEMOUND RD. P.O. BOX 13819 MILWAUKEE, WI 53213

Visit Hal Leonard Online at
www.halleonard.com

SONG STRUCTURE

The songs in this book have different sections, which may or may not include the following:

Intro
This is usually a short instrumental section that "introduces" the song at the beginning.

Verse
This is one of the main sections of a song and conveys most of the storyline. A song usually has several verses, all with the same music but each with different lyrics.

Chorus
This is often the most memorable section of a song. Unlike the verse, the chorus usually has the same lyrics every time it repeats.

Bridge
This section is a break from the rest of the song, often having a very different chord progression and feel.

Solo
This is an instrumental section, often played over the verse or chorus structure.

Outro
Similar to an intro, this section brings the song to an end.

ENDINGS & REPEATS

Many of the songs have some new symbols that you must understand before playing. Each of these represents a different type of ending.

1st and 2nd Endings
These are indicated by brackets and numbers. The first time through a song section, play the first ending and then repeat. The second time through, skip the first ending, and play through the second ending.

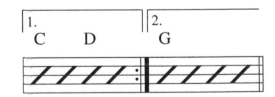

D.S.
This means "Dal Segno" or "from the sign." When you see this abbreviation above the staff, find the sign (𝄋) earlier in the song and resume playing from that point.

al Coda
This means "to the Coda," a concluding section in the song. If you see the words "D.S. al Coda," return to the sign (𝄋) earlier in the song and play until you see the words "To Coda," then skip to the Coda at the end of the song, indicated by the symbol: ⊕.

al Fine
This means "to the end." If you see the words "D.S. al Fine," return to the sign (𝄋) earlier in the song and play until you see the word "Fine."

D.C.
This means "Da Capo" or "from the head." When you see this abbreviation above the staff, return to the beginning (or "head") of the song and resume playing.

CONTENTS

KNOCKIN' ON HEAVEN'S DOOR

Words and Music by
Bob Dylan

Intro
Moderately slow

1. Ma - ma, take this badge off of me;
2. Ma - ma, put my guns in the ground;

I can't use _ it an - y - more _____
I can't shoot them _____ an - y - more. _

It's get - tin' dark, _ too dark _ for me to see;
That long _ black cloud is ___ com - in' down; _

I feel like I'm knock - in' on heav - en's door. _

Chorus

G   D   Am

Knock, knock, knock-in' on heav-en's door. __

G   D   C

Knock, knock, knock-in' on heav-en's door. __

G   D   Am

Knock, knock, knock-in' on heav-en's door. __

To Coda ⊕

G   D   C

Knock, knock, knock-in' on heav-en's door. __

Interlude

G   D   Am   G   D   C

D.S. al Coda

G   D   Am   G   D   C

⊕ **Coda**
Outro

G   D   Am   G   D

1.
C

2.
C   G

YOU BELONG WITH ME

Words and Music by
Taylor Swift and
Liz Rose

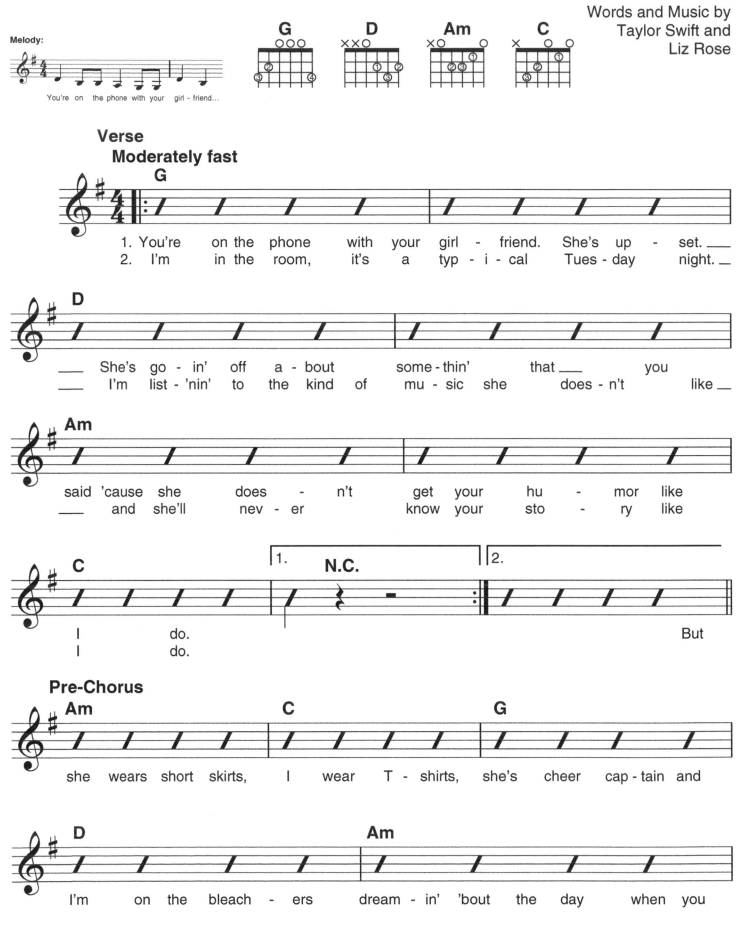

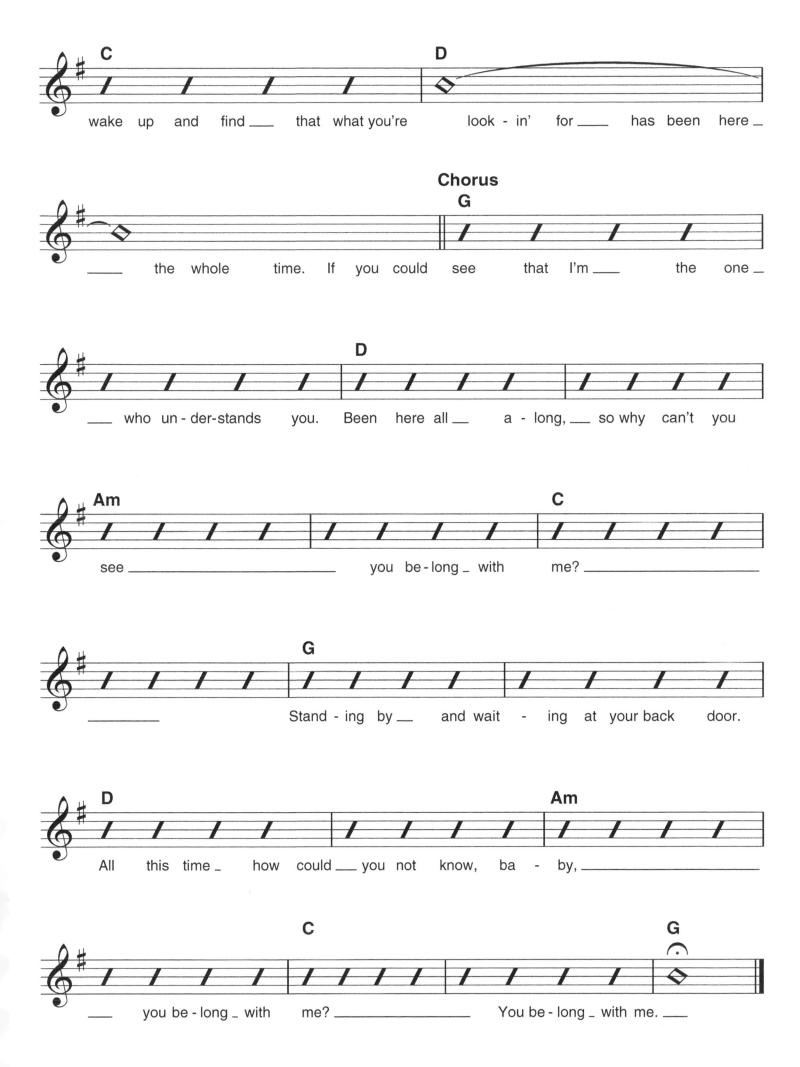

YELLOW SUBMARINE

Words and Music by
John Lennon and Paul McCartney

Verse

G · · · D7 · C · G · Em · Am · C

yel-low sub-ma-rine. 3. And our friends___ are all a - board. Man-y more of them live next

D7 · G · D7 · C · G · D7 G · D7 · G

door. And the band ___ be-gins to ___ play. ___

Chorus

G · D7 · · G

We all live in a yel-low sub-ma-rine, yel-low sub-ma-rine, yel-low sub-ma-rine.

D7 · G

We all live in a yel-low sub-ma-rine, yel-low sub-ma-rine, yel-low sub-ma-rine.

Interlude

D7 · C · G · Em · Am · C

(Instrumental)

D7 · G · D7 · C · G · Em

D.S. al Coda   Coda

Am · C · D7 · G · G

4. As we   yel - low sub-ma-rine.

Outro-Chorus   *Repeat and fade*

G · D7 · · G

We all live in a yel-low sub-ma-rine, yel-low sub-ma-rine, yel-low sub-ma-rine.

ALL OF ME

Words and Music by
John Stephens and Toby Gad

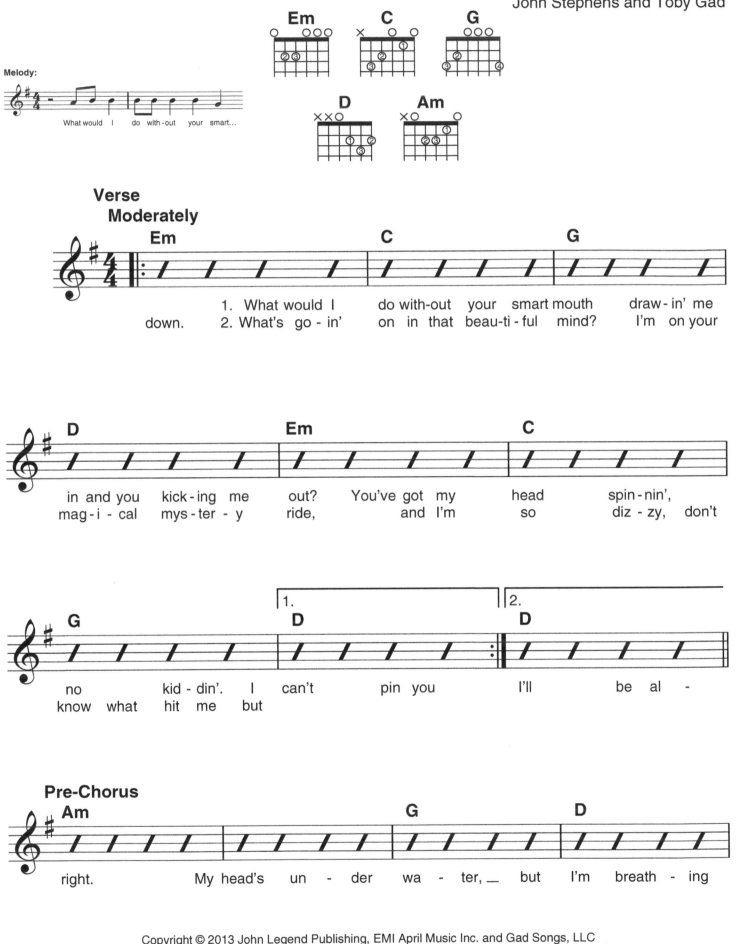

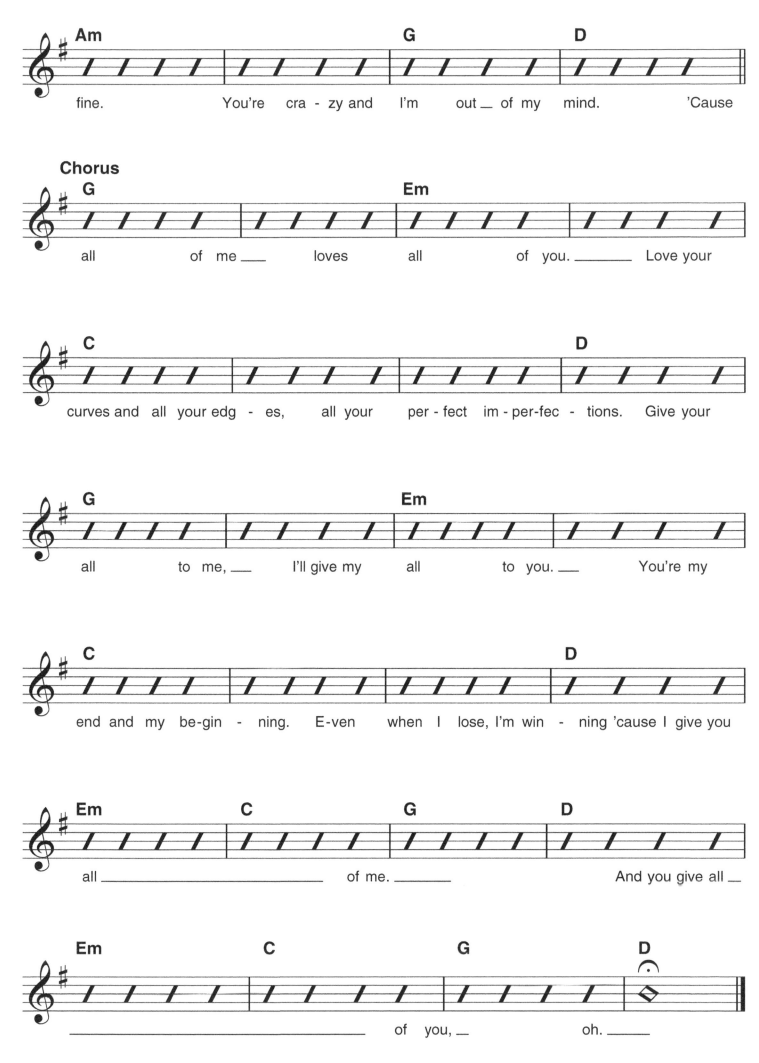

WISH YOU WERE HERE

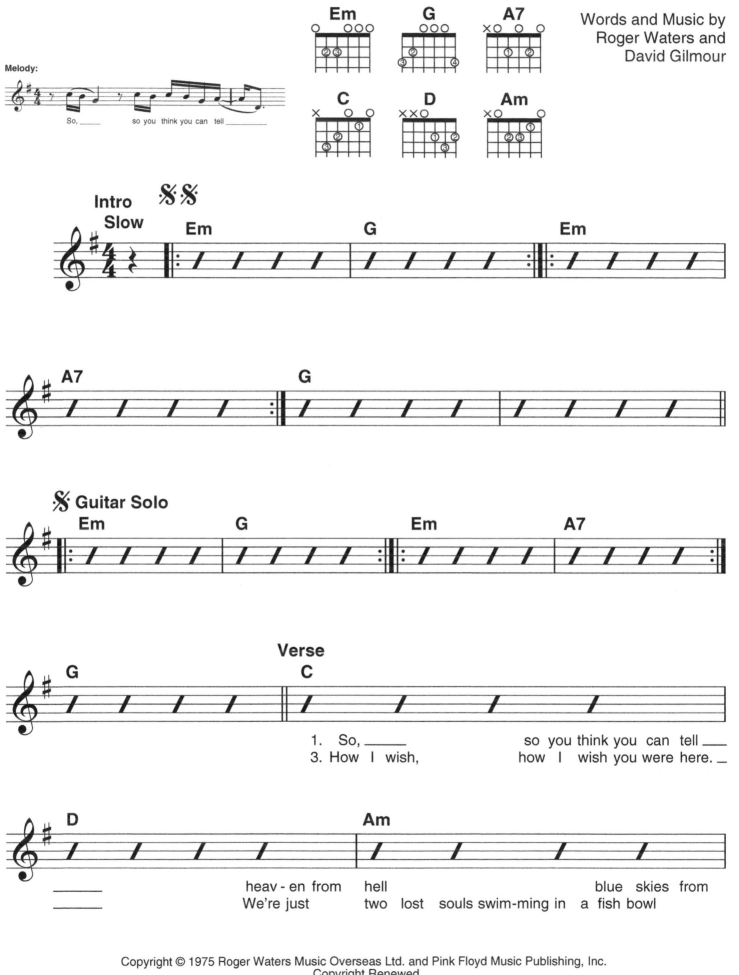

Words and Music by
Roger Waters and
David Gilmour

1. So, _____ so you think you can tell _____
3. How I wish, how I wish you were here. _

_____ heav - en from hell _____ blue skies from
_____ We're just two lost souls swim-ming in a fish bowl

G   D

pain   can you tell a green   field _   from a cold steel

year af - ter year.   Run-ning o-ver the same _ old ground.

To Coda ⊕

C   Am

rail? _____   A smile _ from a veil?   Do you think you can

What have we found?   The same old   fears.   Wish you _   were

Verse

G   C

tell?   2. Did they get you to   trade   your he-roes for

D   Am

ghosts?   Hot   ash - es for   trees?   Hot   air for a

G   D

cool   breeze?   Cold com-fort for   change?   Did you _ ex -

C   Am

change   a walk-on   part in the   war   for a lead _ role in a cage?

D.S. al Coda   ⊕ **Coda**   *D.S.S. and fade on Intro*

(take repeats)   *(take repeats)*

G   G

here.

GET BACK

Words and Music by
John Lennon and Paul McCartney

Intro
Moderately

Verse

1. Jo - jo was a man who thought _ he was a lon - er, but _ he knew it could-n't last. _
2. Sweet Lor-et - ta Mar - tin thought _ she was a wom-an, but she was an - oth - er _ man. _

Jo - jo left his home in Tuc - son Ar - i - zo - na for _
All _ the girls a - round her say _ she's got it com-ing, but

Chorus

some Cal - i - for - nia grass. _
she gets it while she can. _

Get back! _ Get back! _

Get back _ to where you once be - longed. _ Get back! _ Get back! _

Get back _ to where you once be - longed. _ Get back, Jo - jo!
Get back, Loretta!

Guitar Solo

Patience

Words and Music by
W. Axl Rose, Slash, Izzy Stradlin',
Duff McKagan and Steven Adler

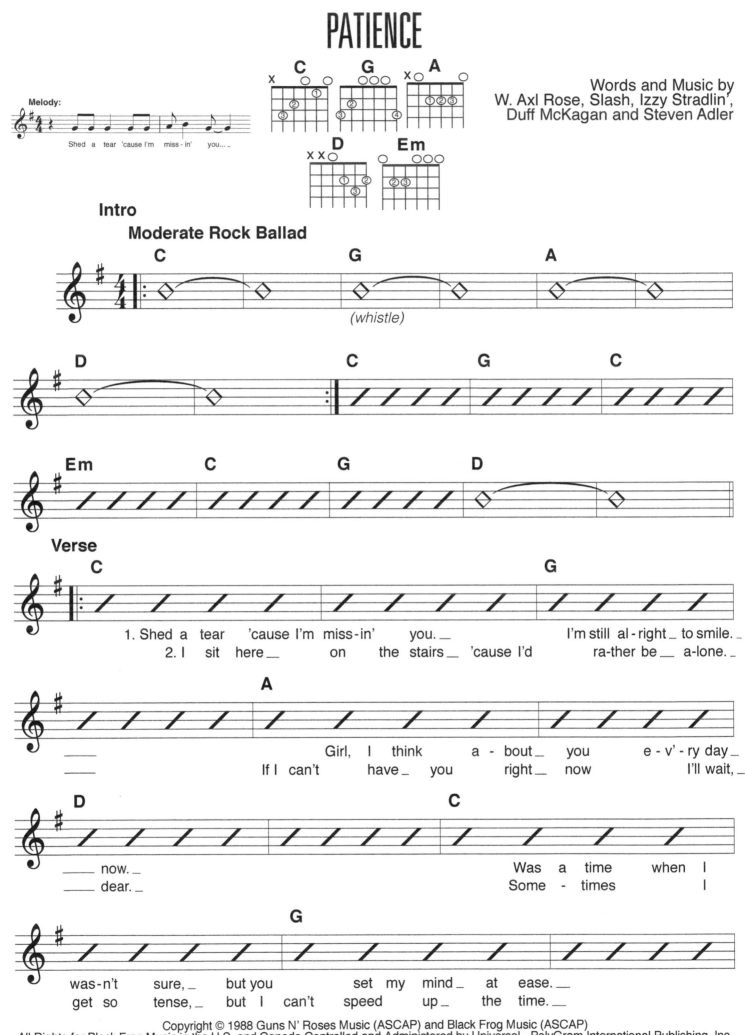

FIRE AND RAIN

Additional Lyrics

2. Won't you look down upon me, Jesus; You got to help me make a stand.
   You've just got to see me through another day.
   My body's aching, and my time is at hand.
   I won't make it any other way.

3. Been walking my mind to an easy time, my back turned towards the sun.
   Lord knows when the cold wind blows, it'll turn your head around.
   Well, there's hours of time on the telephone line to talk about things to come,
   Sweet dreams and flying machines in pieces on the ground.

Evil Ways

Words and Music by
Sonny Henry

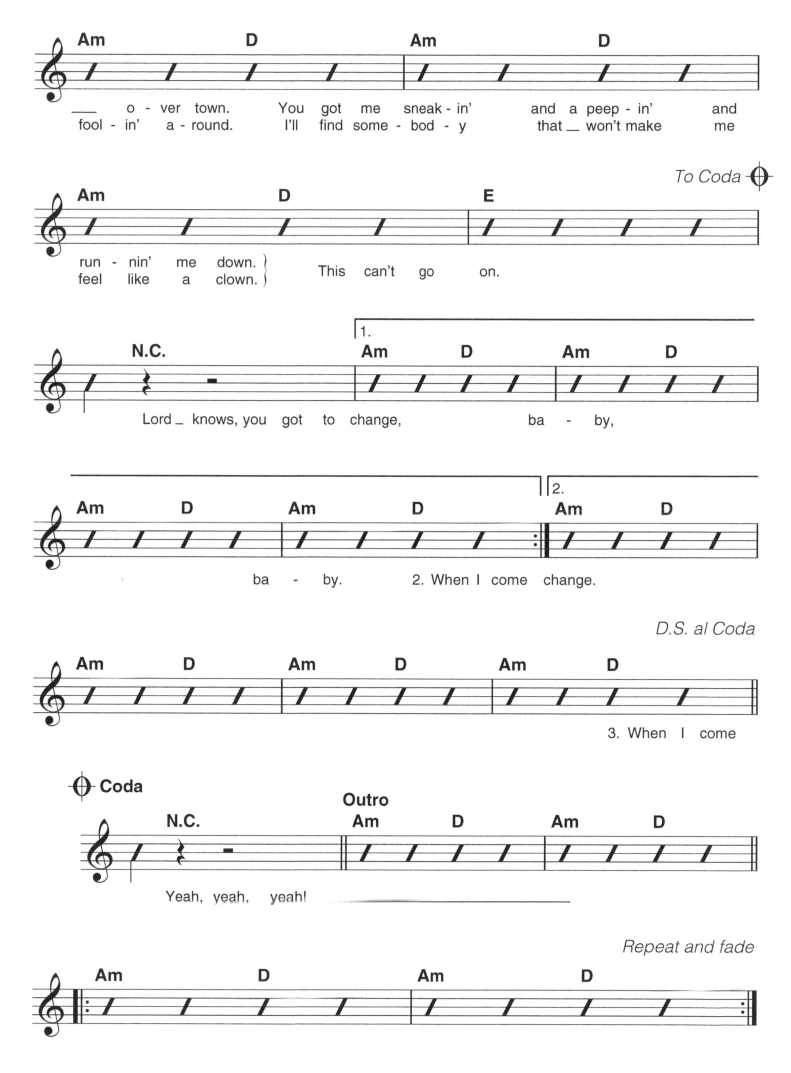

LAY DOWN SALLY

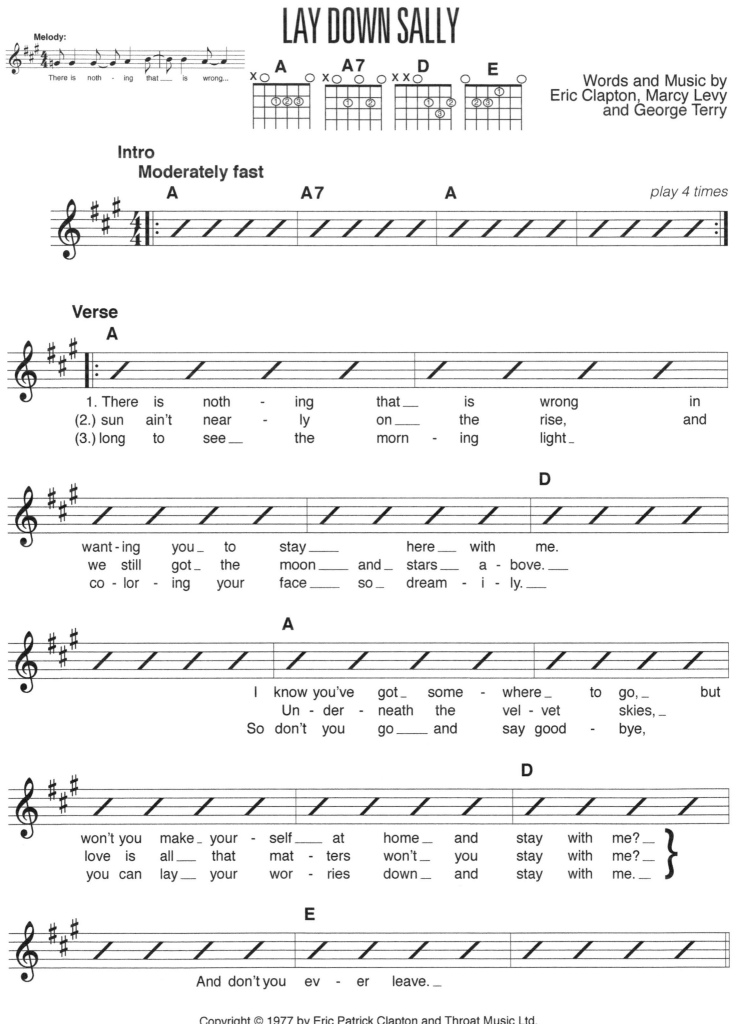

Words and Music by
Eric Clapton, Marcy Levy
and George Terry

Intro
Moderately fast

A   A7   A   *play 4 times*

Verse

A

1. There is noth - ing that ___ is wrong in
(2.) sun ain't near - ly on ___ the rise, and
(3.) long to see ___ the morn - ing light _

D

want - ing you _ to stay ____ here ___ with me.
we still got _ the moon ____ and _ stars ___ a - bove. ___
co - lor - ing your face ____ so _ dream - i - ly. ___

A

I know you've got_ some - where _ to go, _ but
Un - der - neath the vel - vet skies, _
So don't you go ____ and say good - bye,

D

won't you make _ your - self ____ at home _ and stay with me? _
love is all ___ that mat - ters won't _ you stay with me? _
you can lay _ your wor - ries down _ and stay with me. _

E

And don't you ev - er leave. _

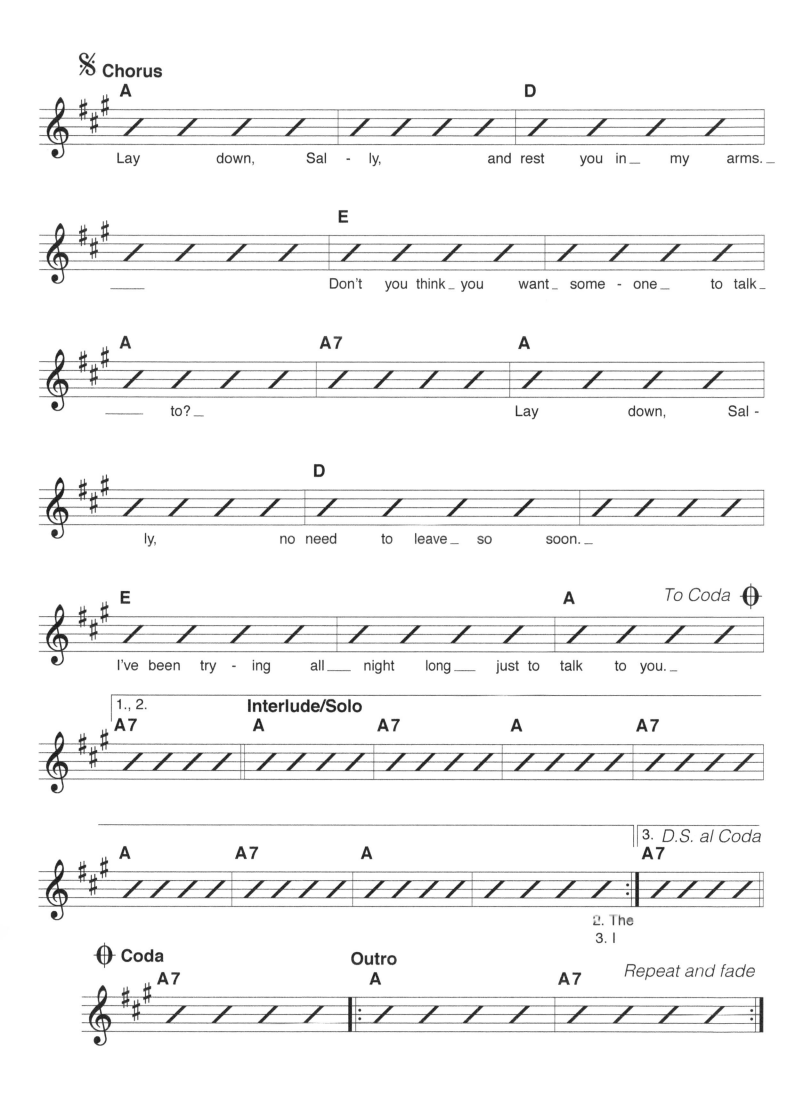

HEY JOE

Words and Music by
Billy Roberts

E

man.
mess-in' 'round town. __
Mex-i-co __ way! __

Yeah!

Al - right! __

C   **G**   **D**   **A**

I'm go-in' down to shoot my old la-dy,   you know I caught her mess-in' round with an -
Ah, yes I did,   I shot her,   you know I caught my old la-dy mess-in' 'round
I'm go-in' way down south, __   way down __ where I __

E   *3rd time, To Coda* ⊕

oth-er man. __ Huh!   And that ain't   too cool.
town. __   And I gave her the gun.   I shot   her! __
__ can be free!   Ain't   no one __ gon-na find me, babe!

Guitar Solo
C   **G**   **D**   **A**   **E**

C   **G**   **D**   **A**   **E**

Interlude
C   **G**   **D**   **A**   **E**   *D.S. al Coda*

⊕ **Coda**
C   **G**   **D**   **A**

Ain't   no hang-man gon-na,   he ain't gon-na put a rope a-round
Hey, __ hey, hey, __ Joe,   you bet-ter run __ on __ down!

E   *Repeat and Fade*

me!   You bet - ter be - lieve __ it right __   now! __ I got-ta go __ now!
Good - bye, ev-'ry - body.   Ow!   *(etc.)*

25

LA BAMBA

By Ritchie Valens

HO HEY

Words and Music by
Jeremy Fraites and
Wesley Schultz

28

Interlude |1. | |2. |

C · · · F C · · · F C · · ·

(Ho!) (Hey!) I be-long with

Chorus

Am · · · G · · · C · · ·

you, you be-long with me. You're my __ sweet - heart. __ I be-long with

Am · · · G · · · F C · · · **Interlude** F

you, you be-long with me. You're my __ sweet... (Ho!

D.S. al Coda

C · · · F C · · · F C · · · F

Hey! Ho! Hey!)

⊕ Coda

C · · · Am · · · G F

She'd be stand-in' next __ to me.

C · · · **Chorus** Am · · · G

I be-long with you, you be-long with me. You're my __ sweet-

C · · · Am · · · G F

- heart. __ I be-long with you, you be-long with me. You're my __ sweet...

Outro

C · · · F C · · · F C · · · F C ◇

(Ho!) Hey! Ho! Hey!)

RAMBLIN' MAN

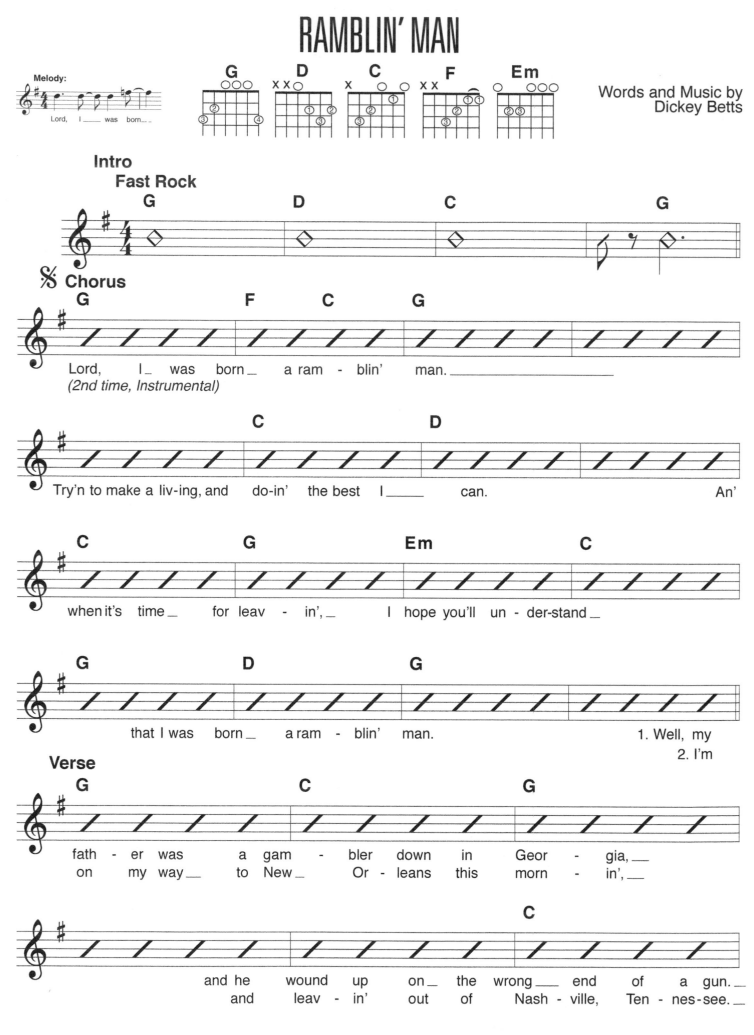

Words and Music by
Dickey Betts

Losing My Religion

Words and Music by
William Berry, Peter Buck,
Michael Mills and Michael Stipe

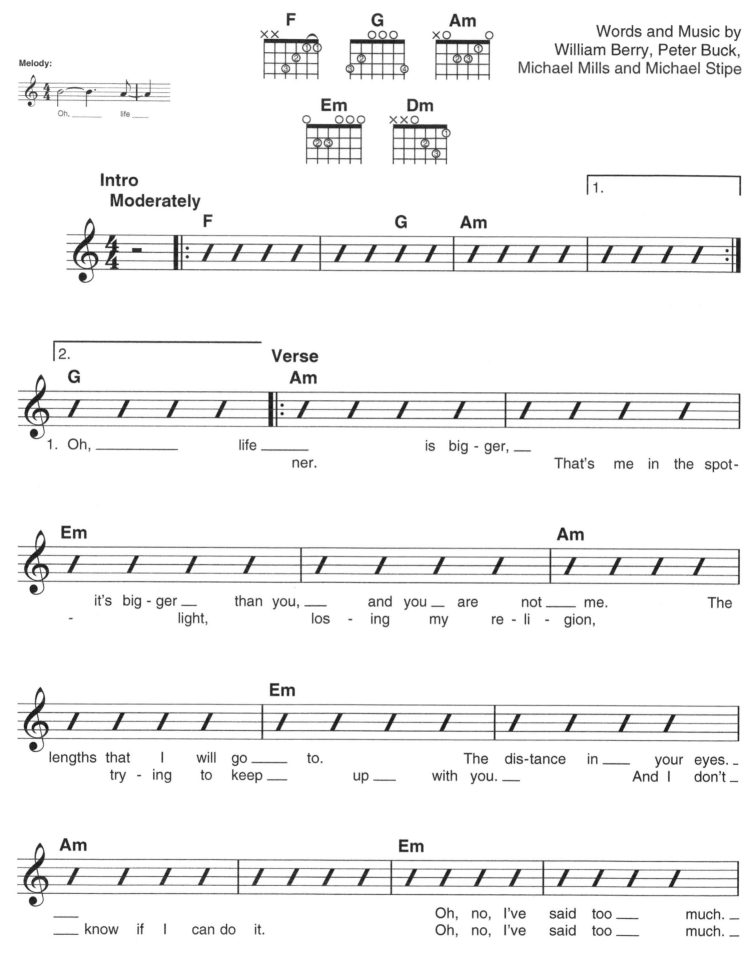

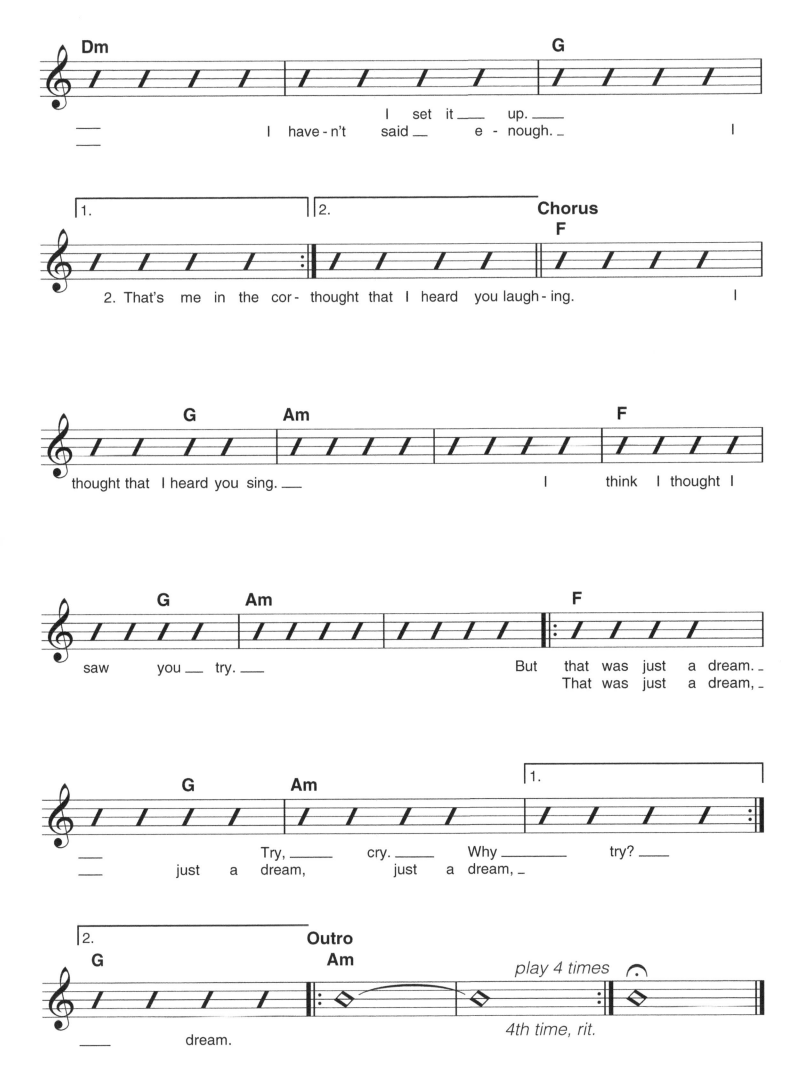

COULD YOU BE LOVED

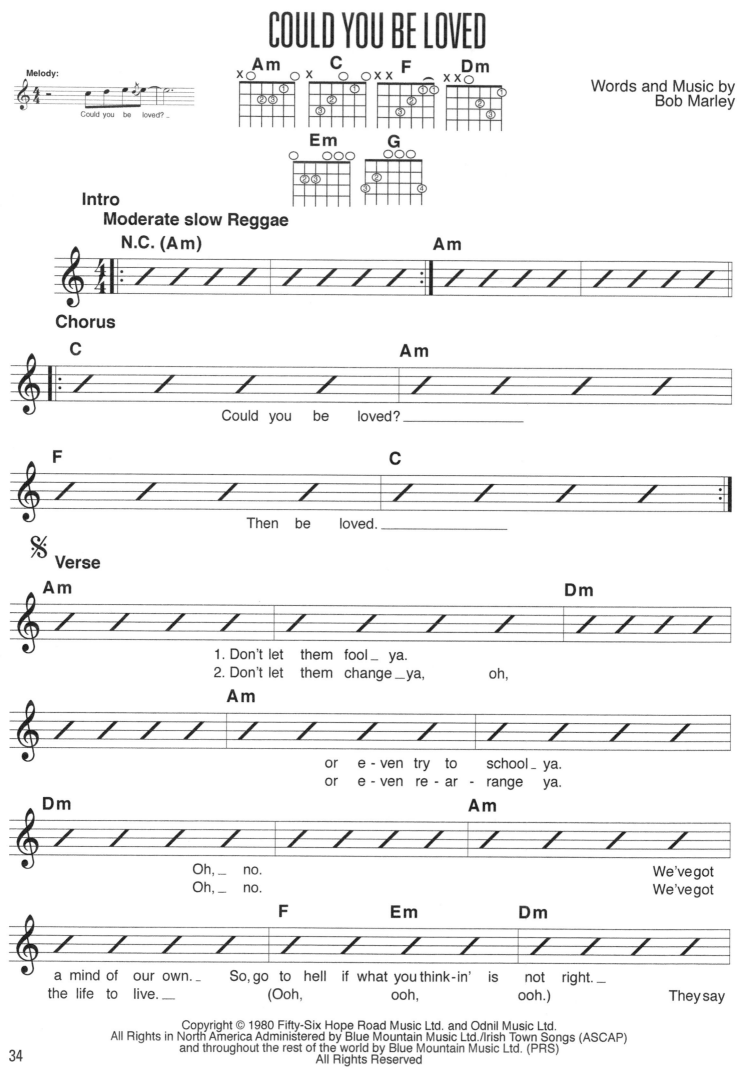

Words and Music by
Bob Marley

SWEET HOME CHICAGO

Words and Music by
Robert Johnson

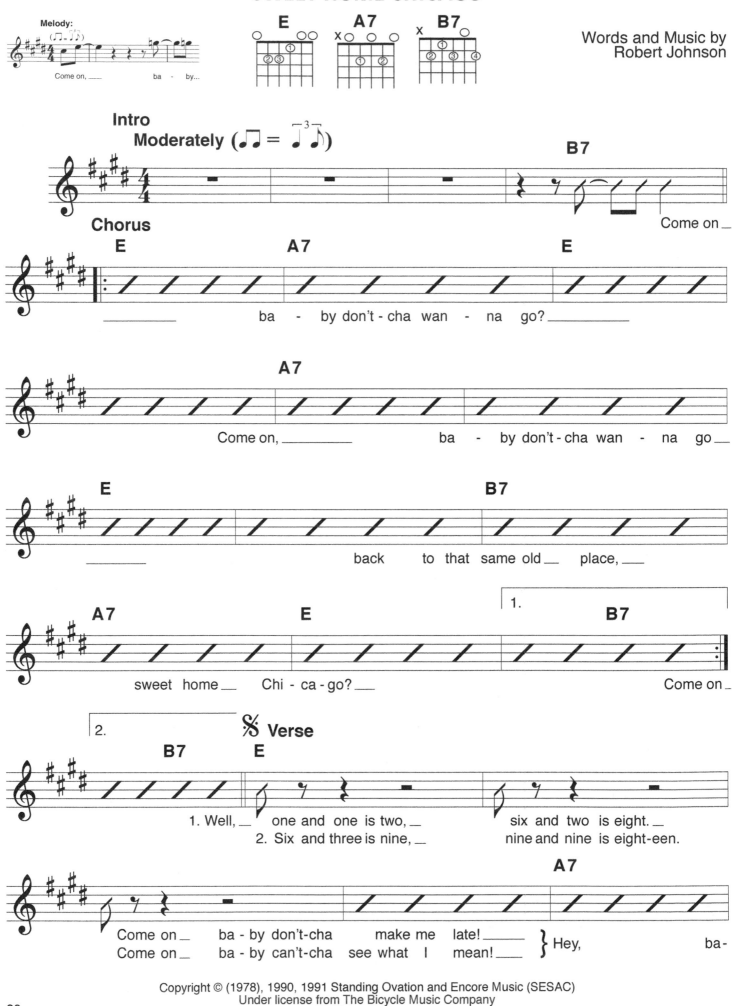

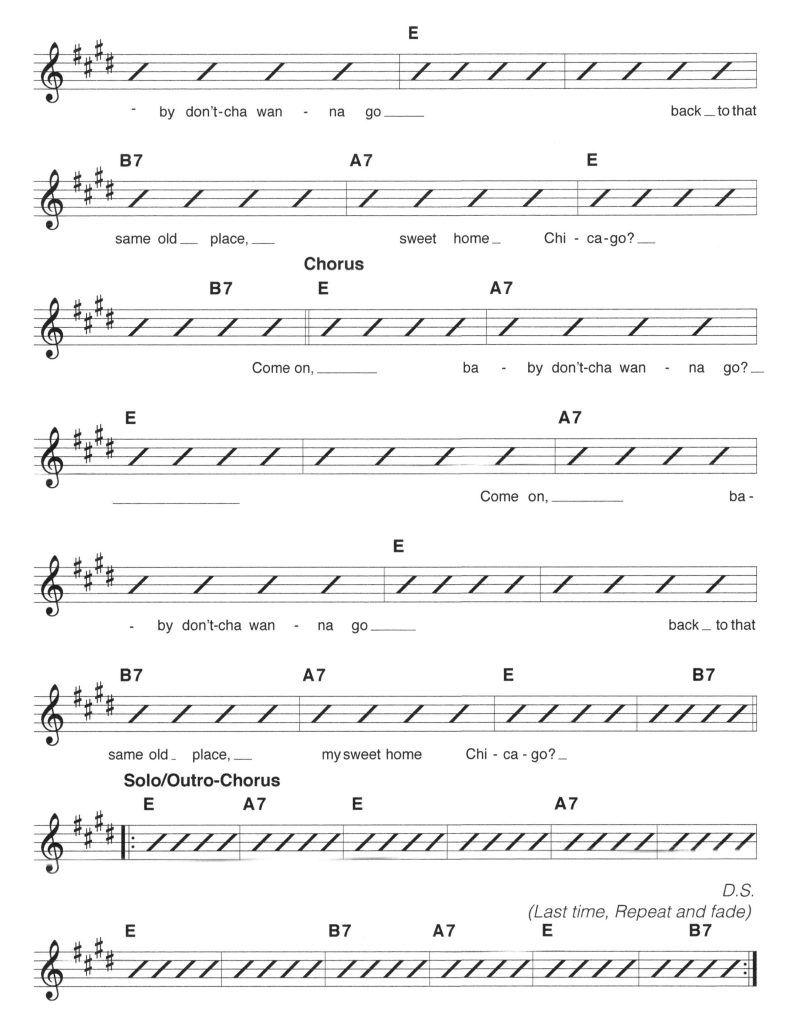

HALLELUJAH

Words and Music by
Leonard Cohen

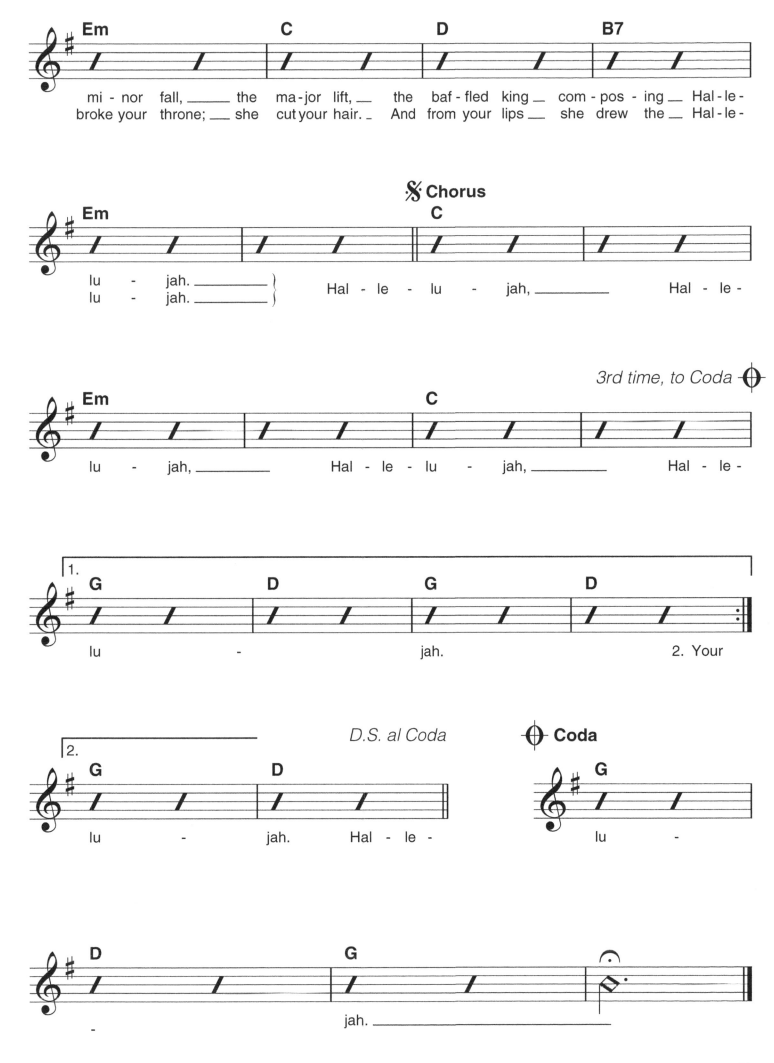

Em   **C**   **D**   **B7**

mi - nor fall, _____ the ma - jor lift, __ the baf - fled king com - pos - ing __ Hal - le -
broke your throne; __ she cut your hair. _ And from your lips __ she drew the __ Hal - le -

※ Chorus

Em   **C**

lu - jah. _____ }
lu - jah. _____ } Hal - le - lu - jah, _____ Hal - le -

3rd time, to Coda ⊕

Em   **C**

lu - jah, _____ Hal - le - lu - jah, _____ Hal - le -

|1.
G   **D**   **G**   **D**

lu - jah.   2. Your

D.S. al Coda   ⊕ **Coda**

|2.
G   **D**   **G**

lu - jah. Hal - le -   lu -

D   **G**

- jah. _____

BLITZKRIEG BOP

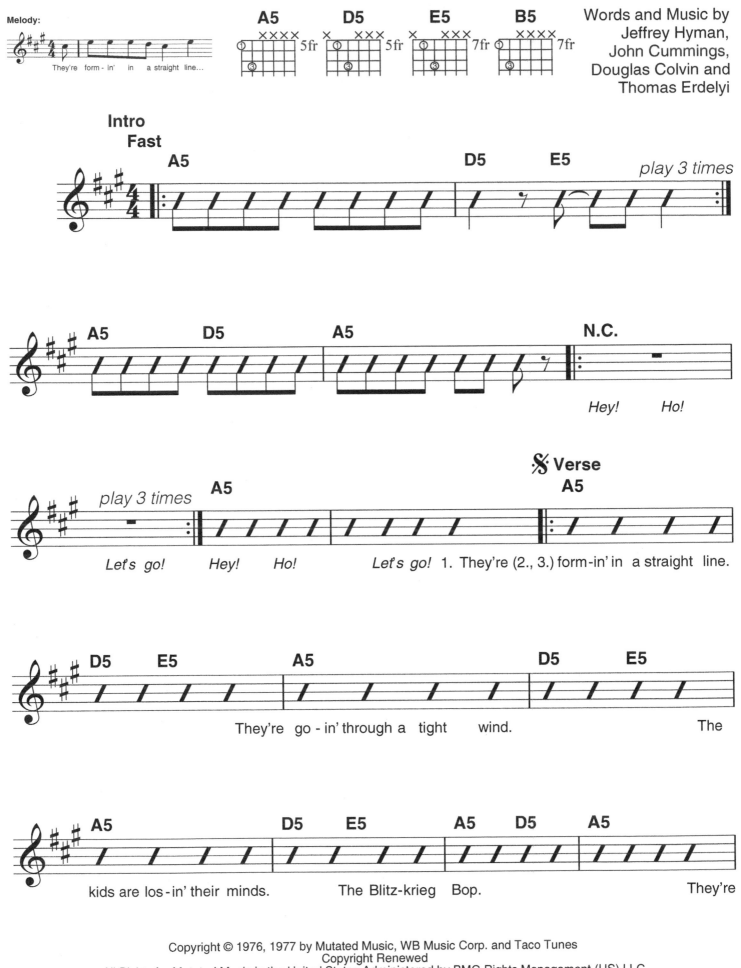

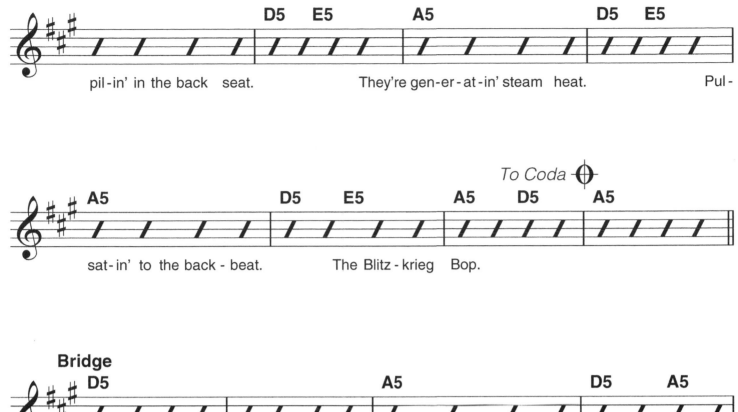

pil-in' in the back seat. They're gen-er-at-in' steam heat. Pul-

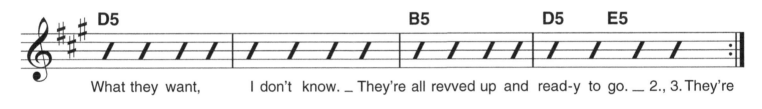

sat-in' to the back - beat. The Blitz-krieg Bop.

Bridge

Hey! Ho! Let's go! Shoot 'em in the back, now.

2nd time, D.S. al Coda

What they want, I don't know. _ They're all revved up and read-y to go. _ 2., 3. They're

Coda   **Outro**

Hey! Ho! Let's go!

Hey! Ho! Let's go!

ABOUT A GIRL

Words and Music by
Kurt Cobain

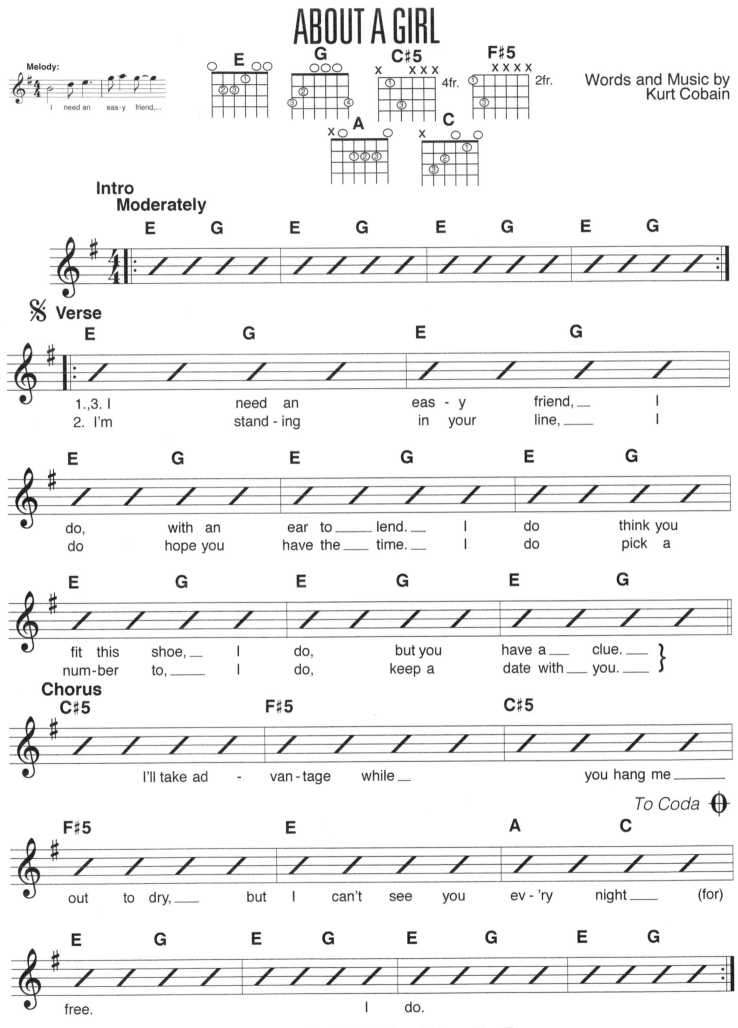

Intro
Moderately

1.,3. I need an eas-y friend, __ I
2. I'm stand-ing in your line, ___ I

do, with an ear to ___ lend. __ I do think you
do hope you have the ___ time. __ I do pick a

fit this shoe, __ I do, but you have a ___ clue. __
num-ber to, ___ I do, keep a date with ___ you. ___

Chorus

I'll take ad - van-tage while ___ you hang me ___

To Coda ⊕

out to dry, ___ but I can't see you ev-'ry night ___ (for)

free. I do.

Guitar Solo

| E | G | E | G | E | G | E | G |

| E | G | E | G | E | G | E | G |

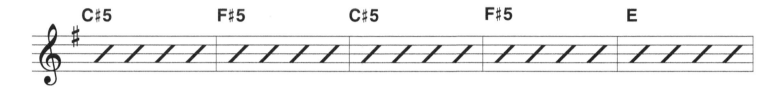

| C#5 | F#5 | C#5 | F#5 | E |

D.S. al Coda

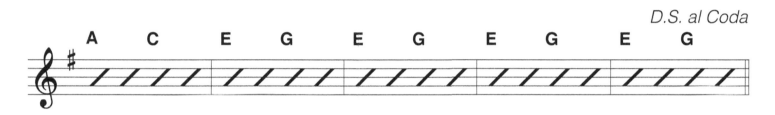

| A | C | E | G | E | G | E | G | E | G |

Coda

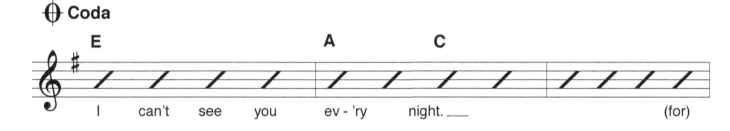

| E | | A | C |

I can't see you ev - 'ry night. ___ (for)

| E | G | E | G | E | G |

free. ___ I do.

| E | G | E | G | E | G |

I do. ___ I

| E | G | E | G | E |

do. ___ I do.

STRUM PATTERNS

The first responsibility of a chord player is to *play the right chord on time*. Keep this in mind as you learn new strumming patterns. No matter how concerned you might be with right-hand strumming, getting to the correct chord with your left hand is more important. If necessary, leave the old chord early in order to arrive at the new chord on time.

That said, here are some suggested strum patterns. Choose one that challenges you, and practice it. Whenever you learn a new chord or progression, try putting it into one of these patterns. Also, try applying these to the songs in this book.

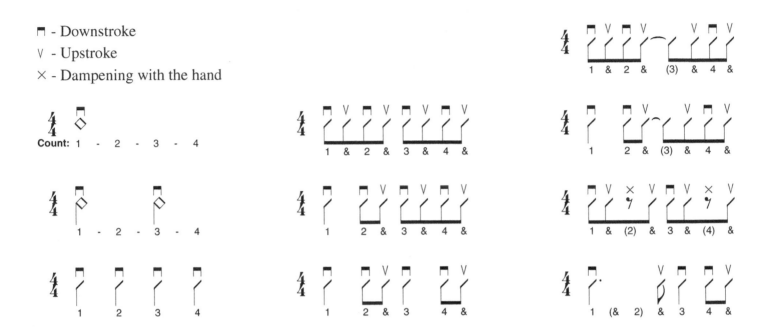

Eighth notes in the above strums may be played even or uneven ("swung") depending on the style of music.

HAL LEONARD GUITAR METHOD
METHOD BOOKS, SONGBOOKS AND REFERENCE BOOKS

THE HAL LEONARD GUITAR METHOD is designed for anyone just learning to play acoustic or electric guitar. It is based on years of teaching guitar students of all ages, and it also reflects some of the best guitar teaching ideas from around the world. This comprehensive method includes: A learning sequence carefully paced with clear instructions; popular songs which increase the incentive to learn to play; versatility – can be used as self-instruction or with a teacher; audio accompaniments so that students have fun and sound great while practicing.

BOOK 1
00699010	Book Only	$9.99
00699027	Book/Online Audio	$14.99
00697341	Book/Online Audio + DVD	$27.99
00697318	DVD Only	$19.99
00155480	Deluxe Beginner Edition (Book, CD, DVD, Online Audio/ Video & Chord Poster)	$22.99

COMPLETE (BOOKS 1, 2 & 3)
00699040	Book Only	$19.99
00697342	Book/Online Audio	$27.99

BOOK 2
00699020	Book Only	$9.99
00697313	Book/Online Audio	$14.99

BOOK 3
00699030	Book Only	$9.99
00697316	Book/Online Audio	$14.99

Prices, contents and availability subject to change without notice.

STYLISTIC METHODS

ACOUSTIC GUITAR
00697347	Method Book/Online Audio	$19.99
00237969	Songbook/Online Audio	$17.99

BLUEGRASS GUITAR
00697405	Method Book/Online Audio	$19.99

BLUES GUITAR
00697326	Method Book/Online Audio (9" x 12")	$16.99
00697344	Method Book/Online Audio (6" x 9")	$15.99
00697385	Songbook/Online Audio (9" x 12")	$16.99
00248636	Kids Method Book/Online Audio	$14.99

BRAZILIAN GUITAR
00697415	Method Book/Online Audio	$17.99

CHRISTIAN GUITAR
00695947	Method Book/Online Audio	$17.99

CLASSICAL GUITAR
00697376	Method Book/Online Audio	$16.99

COUNTRY GUITAR
00697337	Method Book/Online Audio	$24.99

FINGERSTYLE GUITAR
00697378	Method Book/Online Audio	$22.99
00697432	Songbook/Online Audio	$19.99

FLAMENCO GUITAR
00697363	Method Book/Online Audio	$17.99

FOLK GUITAR
00697414	Method Book/Online Audio	$16.99

JAZZ GUITAR
00695359	Book/Online Audio	$22.99
00697386	Songbook/Online Audio	$16.99

JAZZ-ROCK FUSION
00697387	Book/Online Audio	$24.99

R&B GUITAR
00697356	Book/Online Audio	$19.99
00697433	Songbook/CD Pack	$16.99

ROCK GUITAR
00697319	Book/Online Audio	$19.99
00697383	Songbook/Online Audio	$19.99

ROCKABILLY GUITAR
00697407	Book/Online Audio	$19.99

OTHER METHOD BOOKS

BARITONE GUITAR METHOD
00242055	Book/Online Audio	$12.99

GUITAR FOR KIDS
00865003	Method Book 1/Online Audio	$14.99
00697402	Songbook/Online Audio	$12.99
00128437	Method Book 2/Online Audio	$14.99

MUSIC THEORY FOR GUITARISTS
00695790	Book/Online Audio	$22.99

TENOR GUITAR METHOD
00148330	Book/Online Audio	$14.99

12-STRING GUITAR METHOD
00249528	Book/Online Audio	$22.99

METHOD SUPPLEMENTS

ARPEGGIO FINDER
00697352	6" x 9" Edition	$9.99
00697351	9" x 12" Edition	$10.99

BARRE CHORDS
00697406	Book/Online Audio	$16.99

CHORD, SCALE & ARPEGGIO FINDER
00697410	Book Only	$24.99

GUITAR TECHNIQUES
00697389	Book/Online Audio	$16.99

INCREDIBLE CHORD FINDER
00697200	6" x 9" Edition	$7.99
00697208	9" x 12" Edition	$9.99

INCREDIBLE SCALE FINDER
00695568	6" x 9" Edition	$9.99
00695490	9" x 12" Edition	$9.99

LEAD LICKS
00697345	Book/Online Audio	$12.99

RHYTHM RIFFS
00697346	Book/Online Audio	$14.99

SONGBOOKS

CLASSICAL GUITAR PIECES
00697388	Book/Online Audio	$12.99

EASY POP MELODIES
00697281	Book Only	$7.99
00697440	Book/Online Audio	$16.99

(MORE) EASY POP MELODIES
00697280	Book Only	$7.99
00697269	Book/Online Audio	$16.99

(EVEN MORE) EASY POP MELODIES
00699154	Book Only	$7.99
00697439	Book/Online Audio	$16.99

EASY POP RHYTHMS
00697336	Book Only	$10.99
00697441	Book/Online Audio	$16.99

(MORE) EASY POP RHYTHMS
00697338	Book Only	$9.99
00697322	Book/Online Audio	$16.99

(EVEN MORE) EASY POP RHYTHMS
00697340	Book Only	$7.99
00697323	Book/Online Audio	$16.99

EASY POP CHRISTMAS MELODIES
00697417	Book Only	$9.99
00697416	Book/Online Audio	$16.99

EASY POP CHRISTMAS RHYTHMS
00278177	Book Only	$6.99
00278175	Book/Online Audio	$14.99

EASY SOLO GUITAR PIECES
00110407	Book Only	$12.99

REFERENCE

GUITAR PRACTICE PLANNER
00697401	Book Only	$7.99

GUITAR SETUP & MAINTENANCE
00697427	6" x 9" Edition	$16.99
00697421	9" x 12" Edition	$14.99

For more info, songlists, or to purchase these and more books from your favorite music retailer, go to

halleonard.com

HAL•LEONARD®

easy GUITAR play along

Audio Access Included

INCLUDES TAB

The *Easy Guitar Play Along*® series features streamlined transcriptions of your favorite songs. Just follow the tab, listen to the audio to hear how the guitar should sound, and then play along using the backing tracks. Playback tools are provided for slowing down the tempo without changing pitch and looping challenging parts. The melody and lyrics are included in the book so that you can sing or simply follow along.

1. ROCK CLASSICS
Jailbreak • Living After Midnight • Mississippi Queen • Rocks Off • Runnin' Down a Dream • Smoke on the Water • Strutter • Up Around the Bend.
00702560 Book/CD Pack....... $14.99

2. ACOUSTIC TOP HITS
About a Girl • I'm Yours • The Lazy Song • The Scientist • 21 Guns • Upside Down • What I Got • Wonderwall.
00702569 Book/CD Pack....... $14.99

3. ROCK HITS
All the Small Things • Best of You • Brain Stew (The Godzilla Remix) • Californication • Island in the Sun • Plush • Smells Like Teen Spirit • Use Somebody.
00702570 Book/CD Pack....... $14.99

4. ROCK 'N' ROLL
Blue Suede Shoes • I Get Around • I'm a Believer • Jailhouse Rock • Oh, Pretty Woman • Peggy Sue • Runaway • Wake Up Little Susie.
00702572 Book/CD Pack....... $14.99

6. CHRISTMAS SONGS
Have Yourself a Merry Little Christmas • A Holly Jolly Christmas • The Little Drummer Boy • Run Rudolph Run • Santa Claus Is Comin' to Town • Silver and Gold • Sleigh Ride • Winter Wonderland.
00101879 Book/CD Pack......... $14.99

7. BLUES SONGS FOR BEGINNERS
Come On (Part 1) • Double Trouble • Gangster of Love • I'm Ready • Let Me Love You Baby • Mary Had a Little Lamb • San-Ho-Zay • T-Bone Shuffle.
00103235 Book/ Online Audio.........$17.99

9. ROCK SONGS FOR BEGINNERS
Are You Gonna Be My Girl • Buddy Holly • Everybody Hurts • In Bloom • Otherside • The Rock Show • Santa Monica • When I Come Around.
00103255 Book/CD Pack.....$14.99

10. GREEN DAY
Basket Case • Boulevard of Broken Dreams • Good Riddance (Time of Your Life) • Holiday • Longview • 21 Guns • Wake Me up When September Ends • When I Come Around.
00122322 Book/ Online Audio $16.99

11. NIRVANA
All Apologies • Come As You Are • Heart Shaped Box • Lake of Fire • Lithium • The Man Who Sold the World • Rape Me • Smells Like Teen Spirit.
00122325 Book/ Online Audio $17.99

13. AC/DC
Back in Black • Dirty Deeds Done Dirt Cheap • For Those About to Rock (We Salute You) • Hells Bells • Highway to Hell • Rock and Roll Ain't Noise Pollution • T.N.T. • You Shook Me All Night Long.
14042895 Book/ Online Audio........ $17.99

14. JIMI HENDRIX – SMASH HITS
All Along the Watchtower • Can You See Me • Crosstown Traffic • Fire • Foxey Lady • Hey Joe • Manic Depression • Purple Haze • Red House • Remember • Stone Free • The Wind Cries Mary.
00130591 Book/ Online Audio........$24.99

HAL•LEONARD®
www.halleonard.com

Prices, contents, and availability subject to change without notice.

EASY GUITAR
WITH NOTES & TAB

This series features simplified arrangements with notes, tab, chord charts, and strum and pick patterns.

MIXED FOLIOS

00702287	Acoustic	$19.99
00702002	Acoustic Rock Hits for Easy Guitar	$15.99
00702166	All-Time Best Guitar Collection	$19.99
00702232	Best Acoustic Songs for Easy Guitar	$16.99
00119835	Best Children's Songs	$16.99
00703055	The Big Book of Nursery Rhymes & Children's Songs	$16.99
00698978	Big Christmas Collection	$19.99
00702394	Bluegrass Songs for Easy Guitar	$15.99
00289632	Bohemian Rhapsody	$19.99
00703387	Celtic Classics	$16.99
00224808	Chart Hits of 2016-2017	$14.99
00267383	Chart Hits of 2017-2018	$14.99
00334293	Chart Hits of 2019-2020	$16.99
00403479	Chart Hits of 2021-2022	$16.99
00702149	Children's Christian Songbook	$9.99
00702028	Christmas Classics	$8.99
00101779	Christmas Guitar	$14.99
00702141	Classic Rock	$8.95
00159642	Classical Melodies	$12.99
00253933	Disney/Pixar's Coco	$16.99
00702203	CMT's 100 Greatest Country Songs	$34.99
00702283	The Contemporary Christian Collection	$16.99

00196954	Contemporary Disney	$19.99
00702239	Country Classics for Easy Guitar	$24.99
00702257	Easy Acoustic Guitar Songs	$17.99
00702041	Favorite Hymns for Easy Guitar	$12.99
00222701	Folk Pop Songs	$17.99
00126894	Frozen	$14.99
00333922	Frozen 2	$14.99
00702286	Glee	$16.99
00702160	The Great American Country Songbook	$19.99
00702148	Great American Gospel for Guitar	$14.99
00702050	Great Classical Themes for Easy Guitar	$9.99
00275088	The Greatest Showman	$17.99
00148030	Halloween Guitar Songs	$14.99
00702273	Irish Songs	$14.99
00192503	Jazz Classics for Easy Guitar	$16.99
00702275	Jazz Favorites for Easy Guitar	$17.99
00702274	Jazz Standards for Easy Guitar	$19.99
00702162	Jumbo Easy Guitar Songbook	$24.99
00232285	La La Land	$16.99
00702258	Legends of Rock	$14.99
00702189	MTV's 100 Greatest Pop Songs	$34.99
00702272	1950s Rock	$16.99
00702271	1960s Rock	$16.99
00702270	1970s Rock	$24.99
00702269	1980s Rock	$16.99

00702268	1990s Rock	$24.99
00369043	Rock Songs for Kids	$14.99
00109725	Once	$14.99
00702187	Selections from O Brother Where Art Thou?	$19.99
00702178	100 Songs for Kids	$16.99
00702515	Pirates of the Caribbean	$17.99
00702125	Praise and Worship for Guitar	$14.99
00287930	Songs from *A Star Is Born, The Greatest Showman, La La Land*, and More Movie Musicals	$16.99
00702285	Southern Rock Hits	$12.99
00156420	Star Wars Music	$16.99
00121535	30 Easy Celtic Guitar Solos	$16.99
00244654	Top Hits of 2017	$14.99
00283786	Top Hits of 2018	$14.99
00302269	Top Hits of 2019	$14.99
00355779	Top Hits of 2020	$14.99
00374083	Top Hits of 2021	$16.99
00702294	Top Worship Hits	$17.99
00702255	VH1's 100 Greatest Hard Rock Songs	$34.99
00702175	VH1's 100 Greatest Songs of Rock and Roll	$34.99
00702253	Wicked	$12.99

ARTIST COLLECTIONS

00702267	AC/DC for Easy Guitar	$16.99
00156221	Adele – 25	$16.99
00396889	Adele – 30	$19.99
00702040	Best of the Allman Brothers	$16.99
00702865	J.S. Bach for Easy Guitar	$15.99
00702169	Best of The Beach Boys	$16.99
00702292	The Beatles — 1	$22.99
00125796	Best of Chuck Berry	$16.99
00702201	The Essential Black Sabbath	$15.99
00702250	blink-182 — Greatest Hits	$17.99
02501615	Zac Brown Band — The Foundation	$17.99
02501621	Zac Brown Band — You Get What You Give	$16.99
00702043	Best of Johnny Cash	$17.99
00702090	Eric Clapton's Best	$16.99
00702086	Eric Clapton — from the Album Unplugged	$17.99
00702202	The Essential Eric Clapton	$17.99
00702053	Best of Patsy Cline	$17.99
00222697	Very Best of Coldplay – 2nd Edition	$17.99
00702229	The Very Best of Creedence Clearwater Revival	$16.99
00702145	Best of Jim Croce	$16.99
00702278	Crosby, Stills & Nash	$12.99
14042809	Bob Dylan	$15.99
00702276	Fleetwood Mac — Easy Guitar Collection	$17.99
00139462	The Very Best of Grateful Dead	$16.99
00702136	Best of Merle Haggard	$16.99
00702227	Jimi Hendrix — Smash Hits	$19.99
00702288	Best of Hillsong United	$12.99
00702236	Best of Antonio Carlos Jobim	$15.99

00702245	Elton John — Greatest Hits 1970–2002	$19.99
00129855	Jack Johnson	$17.99
00702204	Robert Johnson	$16.99
00702234	Selections from Toby Keith — 35 Biggest Hits	$12.95
00702003	Kiss	$16.99
00702216	Lynyrd Skynyrd	$17.99
00702182	The Essential Bob Marley	$16.99
00146081	Maroon 5	$14.99
00121925	Bruno Mars – Unorthodox Jukebox	$12.99
00702248	Paul McCartney — All the Best	$14.99
00125484	The Best of MercyMe	$12.99
00702209	Steve Miller Band — Young Hearts (Greatest Hits)	$12.95
00124167	Jason Mraz	$15.99
00702096	Best of Nirvana	$16.99
00702211	The Offspring — Greatest Hits	$17.99
00138026	One Direction	$17.99
00702030	Best of Roy Orbison	$17.99
00702144	Best of Ozzy Osbourne	$14.99
00702279	Tom Petty	$17.99
00102911	Pink Floyd	$17.99
00702139	Elvis Country Favorites	$19.99
00702293	The Very Best of Prince	$19.99
00699415	Best of Queen for Guitar	$16.99
00109279	Best of R.E.M.	$14.99
00702208	Red Hot Chili Peppers — Greatest Hits	$17.99
00198960	The Rolling Stones	$17.99
00174793	The Very Best of Santana	$16.99
00702196	Best of Bob Seger	$16.99
00146046	Ed Sheeran	$17.99

00702252	Frank Sinatra — Nothing But the Best	$12.99
00702010	Best of Rod Stewart	$17.99
00702049	Best of George Strait	$17.99
00702259	Taylor Swift for Easy Guitar	$15.99
00359800	Taylor Swift – Easy Guitar Anthology	$24.99
00702260	Taylor Swift — Fearless	$14.99
00139727	Taylor Swift — 1989	$19.99
00115960	Taylor Swift — Red	$16.99
00253667	Taylor Swift — Reputation	$17.99
00702290	Taylor Swift — Speak Now	$16.99
00232849	Chris Tomlin Collection – 2nd Edition	$14.99
00702226	Chris Tomlin — See the Morning	$12.95
00148643	Train	$14.99
00702427	U2 — 18 Singles	$19.99
00702108	Best of Stevie Ray Vaughan	$17.99
00279005	The Who	$14.99
00702123	Best of Hank Williams	$15.99
00194548	Best of John Williams	$14.99
00702228	Neil Young — Greatest Hits	$17.99
00119133	Neil Young — Harvest	$14.99

Prices, contents and availability subject to change without notice.

HAL•LEONARD®

Visit Hal Leonard online at **halleonard.com**